THE MATTRESS CATALOG

BY NASH CONSING

A COMPILATION OF POEMS AND STORIES BY @NASHCONSING FROM INSTAGRAM

Introduction

My name is Nash Consing
and this is a year's worth of internet-published poetry. If you happen to have this book in possession decades after the year 2015, then you should probably visit the app Instagram and go to my account, @nashconsing if it even exists by then.

You'll notice the "To:" at the back of these poems.
This is where you have the option to tear the page out of this book, write something to your crush, your significant other, or even your ex, if you're daring enough. These poems are meant to be shared with the ones you love, or with the ones you used to (or the ones you still do).

The majority of these poems and entries
are about first love experiences. These include poems based on infatuation, falling in love, and heartbreak. These poems are also in chronological order of the time I published them on Instagram, so as you read through you might see changes in the styles that I've written in.

Lastly, I hope you enjoy these poems.
Every single one of them has a personal backstory to me, and I hope that every poem will have the same effect on you as the reader.

A LITTLE BIT
OF WATER
MAKES ME FEEL
LIKE SUMMER
IS ALIVE
AND HAPPINESS
IS REAL

TO:

*IT WAS LATE AT NIGHT
AND THERE WAS
ROMANCE IN THE AIR
IT WOULD HAVE BEEN
THE PERFECT NIGHT
EXCEPT YOU WEREN'T
THERE*

TO:

IT'S IMPOSSIBLE

FOR ME

TO NOT FALL IN LOVE

THE MOMENT

OUR EYES MEET

BECAUSE ALL OF

A SUDDEN

MY HALF-FILLED

HEART

MAGICALLY FEELS

COMPLETE

TO:

SHE HAD EYES

LIKE THE SEA

AND THE PERSONALITY

OF GOLD

ONLY IF SHE COULD

RELEASE

HER INSECURITIES

EVERYONE COULD SEE

HER BEAUTY UNFOLD

TO:

I'M NOT SAYING THAT

I WANT YOU BACK

BUT IF I'M GOING TO

SURVIVE THE NIGHT

THEN I'LL NEED

YOUR PRESENCE

TO KEEP ME IN TACT

TO:

I TOLD MYSELF

I NEEDED TO BE SQUARE

IF I WANTED TO MOVE ON

THIS TIME

BUT RIGHT NOW

IT'S RATHER HARD

BECAUSE YOU'RE

RUNNING CIRCLES

THROUGH MY MIND

TO:

EVERY SINGLE MOMENT

I AM WITH YOU

I NEVER QUESTION

THE FACT

THAT MY DREAMS

HAVE COME TRUE

TO:

THEY SAY

THE SHORTER

THE WORDS

THE SWEETER

BUT BABY

I'D WRITE A BOOK

ABOUT YOU

TO SHOW YOU

THAT I'M A KEEPER

TO:

WE ARE LIKE

THE HANDS OF A

CLOCK

RIGHT AFTER

IT STRIKES TEN

BECAUSE IF YOU

KEEP PATIENT

SOONER OR LATER

WE WILL MEET AGAIN

TO:

PICKED

I PICKED YOU

LIKE A FLOWER

AND FOR A WHILE

YOU WERE INSPRIRING

BUT FLOWERS

ARE MEANT TO BE TIED

TO THEIR ROOTS

BECAUSE NOW

YOU ARE DYING

19

TO:

MY EYES HAVE

TURNED RED

AND MY SKIN

IS CREEPING BLUE

BECAUSE YOU'RE

TAKING MY BREATH
AWAY

AND I'M DYING

FOR A PERSON LIKE
YOU

TO:

YOU MAY BE

THE WORLD

AS I AM JUST

A GRAIN OF SAND

BUT I WILL ALWAYS

BE A PART OF YOU,

NO MATTER WHAT

YOUR LIFE

HAS PLANNED

TO:

I DON'T LONG

FOR THE STARS

ON OVERCASTED SKIES

BECAUSE THE NIGHT

IS STILL ADMIRABLE

THROUGH THE BEAUTY

OF YOUR EYES

TO:

I'VE ALWAYS FELT

TIED TO YOU

EVEN THOUGH YOU'VE

WALLED ME AWAY

BECAUSE THE ROPE

THAT TIES MY HEART

TO YOURS

IS LONG ENOUGH

TO TRICK MY HEAD

TO STAY

TO:

ON A SCALE OF

ONE TO TEN,

YOU MAY AS WELL

BE INFINITY

BECAUSE SINCE THE

FIRST DAY I MET YOU,

MY HEART'S BEEN

IN YOUR CAPTIVITY

TO:

MY ROOM IS FILLED

WITH LETTERS

THAT I'LL PROBABLY

NEVER SEND

BECAUSE I WANT YOU

BACK SO BADLY

BUT INSTEAD

I JUST PRETEND

TO:

I'VE WRITTEN A HUNDRED

POEMS ABOUT YOU

BUT YOU'RE

<u>NEVER</u> COMING BACK

AND I'LL DREAM

OF ALL OUR MEMORIES

BUT WHEN YOU

THINK OF ME

YOUR MIND

WILL PROBABLY

TURN BLACK

TO:

IN OUR EXISTENCE

WE CAN BE AS SMALL

AS A WATER MOLECULE

OR AS BIG

AS THE GALAXIES

BUT I'LL STILL LOVE YOU

MORE THAN ALL

THE STARS IN THE SKY

COMBINED WITH

ALL THE DROPLETS

IN THE SEAS

TO:

I'M SURROUNDED

BY ALL THESE PEOPLE

THAT I KNOW

BUT NEVER HAVE I FELT

SO LONELY

BECAUSE IN A WORLD

FULL OF NUMBERS

YOU WERE

SUPPOSED TO BE

MY ONE AND ONLY

TO:

THERE'S A DIFFERENCE
BETWEEN LUST AND LOVE
BUT EITHER WAY
I'M CHASING YOU
AND EVEN THOUGH
I WON'T BE YOURS
TOMORROW
TONIGHT I'LL ENJOY
THE VIEW

TO:

I WANT TO CALL YOU

A LIAR

EVEN THOUGH NONE OF THIS

WAS YOUR FAULT

BUT YOU PROMISED ME

CONTINUATION

AND INSTEAD WE'VE

COME TO A HALT

TO:

I'M LOST IN THE

SEA OF LOVE

BECAUSE YOUR CURRENT

IS PULLING ME

FROM THE SHORE

AND MAYBE I MIGHT BE

A HOPELESS ROMANTIC

BUT I'LL ALWAYS

BE SWIMMING BACK

FOR MORE

TO:

LOVE TASTES LIKE

THE BEER

WHEN I MET YOU

THE WINE

WHEN YOU WERE MINE

AND THE WHISKEY

WHEN YOU LEFT ME

BECAUSE LOVE IS DISORIENTING

LIKE THE ALCOHOL

I CONSUMED

WHETHER IT FILLED ME UP

OR LEFT ME EMPTY

TO:

I WAS LIKE
THE SUN
IN THE WINTER;
EVEN ON OUR
COLD DAYS
I'D STILL
FALL FOR YOU

TO:

I HAVE TO LISTEN

TO YOUR OLD

VOICEMAILS

ON THE PHONE

JUST TO MAKE

ME FEEL

LIKE YOUR HEART

IS STILL MY HOME

TO:

WE HAVE

24 HOURS

IN THE DAY

AND I'VE SPENT

EVERY SECOND

WISHING THAT

YOU'D STAY

TO:

THERE ARE THINGS

*WE'LL NEVER KNOW
AND PLACES*

WE'LL NEVER SEE

BUT I'LL FIND

THE SECRETS OF

THE WORLD

AS LONG AS YOU

STAY WITH ME

TO:

I USED TO THINK

THAT WE WERE LEGENDS

BECAUSE

THE BEST STARS

NEVER DIE

BUT THAT WAS BEFORE

WE TURNED INTO

DYING GASES,

JUST BURNING UP IN THE SKY

TO:

YOU WERE JUST

A GHOST

TRAPPED

INSIDE MY HEAD

BECAUSE I KEPT

FEELING A LOVE

IN A TIME

WHERE OUR

RELATIONSHIP

WAS LONG DEAD

TO:

I'D FOLLOW YOU

INTO A FIRE

AS LONG AS I'D

GET TO BE WITH YOU

AND I'D DROWN MYSELF

IN THE OCEAN

JUST TO REMEMBER

HOW YOUR EYES

SHINED BLUE

TO:

YOU TOOK

THE LEFT

SO I CHOSE

THE RIGHT

BUT I KNEW WE'D BE

TOGETHER AGAIN

WHEN YOU CIRCLED

BACK INTO MY SIGHT

TO:

IT'S LIKE WE MADE

ORIGAMI BOATS

AND SET THEM OUT

TO THE SEA

WITH THE SAME

PROBABILITY

THAT YOU'D END UP

STAYING WITH ME

TO:

IT COULD BE FOREVER

UNTIL I SEE YOU

ONCE MORE

BUT IT ALWAYS SEEMS

LIKE I'LL BE WITH

YOU SOON

BECAUSE I'M WITH YOU

EVERY NIGHT

LIKE HOW THE STARS

ACCOMPANY THE MOON

TO:

WE'RE BOTH

SITTING ALONE

JUST ON

DIFFERENT BEDS

BECAUSE WE'VE TRIED

TO MOVE ON

FROM EACH OTHER

BUT NOW WE JUST LIE

IN EACH OTHERS'

HEADS

TO:

**TRYING TO
LOVE YOU
IS LIKE SEEING
A TRAILER
BUT NEVER
WATCHING
THE MOVIE**

TO:

SOME DAYS WHEN

I WITNESS DYING SUNS

I ASK MYSELF

SHOULD I EVEN HOLD ON?

BUT YOU REMIND ME

THAT EVERY MORNING

THE SUN RISES

EVEN AFTER THINGS

HAVE GONE WRONG

TO:

HE STOPPED PRAYING

TO GOD

WHEN SHE WALKED

HER LOVE

INTO HIS HEART

AND MAYBE THAT'S WHY

HE FELT SO EMPTY

WHEN SHE TOOK HER LOVE

AND LEFT

TO:

WE WROTE OUR

PROMISES IN

PENCIL

AND FLEW THEM

ON PAPER PLANES

IN HOPES THAT

WE COULD

FLY FOREVER

TO:

WE'RE ALL BORN

WITH A DISEASE

AND WE ALL

DIE WITH A CURE

BECAUSE EVEN IF IT

TAKES US HALF

OUR LIVES

EVENTUALLY WE ALL

FIND WHAT WE'RE

SEARCHING FOR

TO:

You weren't all that
I had;
I had friends, family,
love.
You were the only thing
I ever lost,
And maybe that's why
I felt like a child
after it was all over.

TO:

PLAY

WE WERE

JUST

A SINGLE;

WE COULD

HAVE BEEN

AN ALBUM

81

TO:

MARIE

MAYBE I'LL JUST BE

A BOY YOU USED TO LOVE

OR MAYBE I'LL BE

SOMETHING MORE

WE CAN NEVER PREDICT

THE FUTURE

BUT YOUR HEART

IS SOMETHING

I WILL ALWAYS

BE SEARCHING FOR

TO:

LIGHTNING STRIKES

INTO MY VEINS

THE MOMENT

YOU GLANCE

INTO MY HEAD

BECAUSE YOUR EYES

ARE SO ELECTRIFYING

THAT YOU LEAVE

MY HEARTBEAT

DEAD

TO:

I'VE LISTENED TO ALL

THESE STUPID LOVE

SONGS THAT HAVE

PROMISED US FOREVER

WHEN WE'VE RUN

THROUGH

HELL AND BACK

AND STILL WE'RE

NOT TOGETHER

TO:

*IT JUST SUCKS BECAUSE
I'M STARTING TO FORGET
THE SOUND OF YOUR VOICE
AND THE WAY YOUR HANDS
FELT AROUND MY SKIN*

*BECAUSE BABY WE WERE
NEVER ABLE TO WORK OUT
BUT OH GOD
THE THINGS WE
COULD HAVE BEEN*

TO:

I never liked art
until I studied the scars
on your skin.

I never liked sculptures
until I felt the curves on
your body.

I never liked poetry
until I read into all of
your insecurities.

I never liked art
until you gave me every
form of being beautiful.

TO:

TONIGHT I'LL BE RUNNING

AFTER STRANGERS

AND KISSING NAMES

I'LL NEVER KNOW

'CAUSE I JUST

WANT TO BE FREE

IN A WORLD THAT

ALWAYS TELLS ME

WHERE TO GO

TO:

"Tell me you love me,"
even though she knew he wouldn't respond.
"Tell me that it's all going to be okay,"
even though he was the one who ruined her.
"You told me that your lips belonged to me,"
even though he was already kissing other girls.
"Baby, you made me,"
even though he was the one who destroyed her.

"I still love you."

Even though he no longer did.

TO:

WHEN YOU KISSED ME
YOU SAID I HAD
GIVEN YOU A DISEASE
BUT I NEVER
MEANT FOR IT
TO DESTROY US

TO:

OUR WORLD HAS BECOME

DULL AND RAINY

BUT ONE DAY THE CLOUDS

WILL DISSOLVE AWAY

AND AT THAT MOMENT

YOU WILL BE GREATFUL

THAT YOUR HEART

HAS CONVINCED YOU

TO STAY

TO:

YOU MAKE ME FEEL

SO ALIVE

BUT YOU'RE KILLING

ME AS WELL

BECAUSE YOUR EYES

ARE MY HEAVENS

BUT YOU'RE TREATING

ME LIKE HELL

TO:

BABY I'M IN LOVE

WITH YOUR THOUGHTS

THAT ARE DEEPER

THAN POETRY

AND NOW YOU'VE GOT ME

PRAYING EVERY DAY

TO BE WITH YOU

LIKE A ROSARY

TO:

WRITING ABOUT YOU

USED TO BE THERAPY

BUT RECENTLY

I'VE TAKEN

AN OVERDOSE

AND NOW IT'S 4 A.M.'S

THINKING ABOUT US

BUT WISHING THAT

I'M IN COMATOSE

TO:

EVEN THOUGH

FATE HAS TOLD US

COUNTLESS TIMES

THAT WE WERE NEVER

MEANT TO BE

THE BOTTOM OF

MY HEART

WILL ALWAYS HOPE

THAT YOU WILL

BE SEARCHING FOR ME

TO:

*IF SOMEONE EVER
TOLD ME TO STOP
CHASING MY DREAMS
THEN I'D HAVE TO
STOP CHASING YOU*

TO:

My greatest fear as a
poet that feeds
off of live emotions
is when I am
no longer in love,
or when my heart
is not broken,
or even when
I cannot lust
over strangers.
I am just existing.
I am not writing.
I am not *living.*

TO:

WE MADE OUR WISHES

ON THE SAME

SHOOTING STARS

BUT WE PRAYED

FOR DIFFERENT THINGS;

YOU WANTED TO

FLY AWAY

WHILE I WISHED

TO RECONNECT

OUR STRINGS

WOULD YOU STILL CONSIDER TO BE MY VALENTINE EVEN IF MY WORDS ARE CORNIER THAN ON THE COB?

TO:

CUPID SHOT

HIS ARROW

AND MY OH MY,

HE SHOT IT WELL

'CAUSE RECENTLY

I'VE BEEN INFATUATED

WITH YOU

LIKE I'VE BEEN

PUT UNDER A SPELL

TO:

SOME PEOPLE CHASE

AFTER MONEY

SOME EVEN LUST

AFTER FAME

BUT I JUST WANTED

YOU TO BE MINE

EVEN BEFORE I KNEW

YOUR NAME

TO:

EVEN AFTER

THE ROSES ARE DEAD

AND THE SKIES ARE

NO LONGER BLUE

THERE WILL

BE NOBODY

TO ME

THAT'S MORE

COLORFUL THAN YOU

TO:

LET'S WATCH SOME

BEAUTIFUL SUNSETS

AND SHARE

A COUPLE DRINKS

BECAUSE LIFE IS JUST

A BIGGER TITANIC

AND I WANT TO LOVE YOU

BEFORE IT SINKS

TO:

IF LIFE WAS A
MATH TEST,
I'D CONSTANTLY BE
GUESSING 'C'
BUT IF THERE'S ONE
THING THAT I KNOW
FOR SURE,
IT'S THAT I WANT YOU
TO BE WITH ME

TO:

I'M LIVING IN THE
TRANSITION FROM THE
SETTING OF THE SUN
TO THE RISING
OF THE MOON
AND AS THE YOUNG NIGHT
MAY SEEM LONELY NOW
I KNOW THAT I'LL FALL
IN LOVE WITH THE LIGHT
AGAIN AND VERY SOON

TO:

AS I GO ABOUT THE DAY

I SEE A SKY

FULL OF STARS

BUT WHEN I SEE YOU

I FEEL THE SUN

IF YOU'D ASK HOW LONG

I'VE BEEN BLINDED

BY YOUR BEAUTY

I'D TELL YOU

IT'S BEEN SINCE DAY ONE

TO:

I DIDN'T KNOW WHAT
LOVE AT FIRST SIGHT WAS
UNTIL I SAW YOU
AND NOW I SPEND EVERY
DAY AND EVERY NIGHT
WONDERING WHEN OUR
FIRST HELLO
IS DUE

TO:

VALENTINA

> *YOU DON'T HAVE TO*
> *LIKE ME*
> *I DON'T CARE IF YOU'RE*
> *NOT MINE*
> *BUT MAYBE FOR TODAY*
> *WOULD YOU BE*
> *MY VALENTINE?*

TO:

YOU LOVED ME

BUT YOU LOVED

TIME MORE

BECAUSE YOU WERE

STILL CHECKING

YOUR WATCH

AS I WAS

WALKING OUT THE DOOR

TO:

THE IDEA OF US

HATING ONE ANOTHER

IS A COMMON

MISCONCEPTION

I'M SURE YOU STILL

LOVE ME

BUT OUR HEARTS

HAVE MOVED ON

IN A DIFFERENT DIRECTION

TO:

WHEN LOVERS LEAVE

ONE ANOTHER,

THEY NEVER SAY

GOODBYE

BUT IT'S BEEN MONTHS

SINCE I LAST SAW YOU

AND I STILL LOOK

FOR YOU IN THE SKY

TO:

I SEE YOU IN THE FACES

OF STRANGERS

BUT I SEE A STRANGER

IN YOU

AND NOW WHEN I WRITE

ALL THESE POEMS

I CAN'T TELL IF

THE ROSES ARE RED

OR IF

THE VIOLETS ARE BLUE

TO:

After a day, I was whispering,

"Marie, Marie, Marie, don't you ever leave me."

After a month, I was pleading,

"Marie, Marie, Marie, don't you still have needs for me?"

After a year, I told myself,

"Marie, Marie, Marie, I hope your heart still bleeds for me."

As Marie, Marie, Marie,

no longer wanted a thing from me.

TO:

I FELL IN LOVE WITH

A GIRL NAMED WEEKEND

AND QUICKLY SHE BECAME

MY ESCAPE AT LAST

BUT AFTER TWO LATE NIGHTS

OF SHARING MEMORIES,

SHE STOOD UP FROM MY BED

AND TOLD ME

THAT OUR TIME TOGETHER

HAD PASSED

TO:

WHEN YOU ENTERED

THE ROOM

YOU MADE MY HEART PULSE

AS LOUDLY AS A

BEATING DRUM

AND I KNEW YOU HEARD

THE SOUND I MADE

BECAUSE YOU SMILED

AT ME WITH THE SPEED

OF A SINGLE STRUM

TO:

*SHE STOPPED
SMILING
IN PICTURES
BECAUSE A
BLANK FACE
HELD A LOT MORE
TRUTH
THAN A FORGED
SIGNATURE*

TO:

**BEFORE I KNEW IT,
I SOLD MY HEART
TO A GIRL MORE
BEAUTIFUL
THAN A WORK
OF ART**

TO:

ACTING NORMAL

WITH A PERSON LIKE YOU

IS EASIER

SAID THAN DONE

BECAUSE YOU'VE MADE

MY HEARTBEAT RAPID

AND MY VISION BLURRY

EVER SINCE DAY ONE

TO:

AS DISTANT AS

I MAY SEEM,

OR AS FAR AWAY

FATE HAS SEPARATED

US TO BE

I HOPE YOU'RE

STILL HAPPY

REGARDLESS OF THE

WAY YOU THINK OF ME

TO:

SOMETIMES YOU
FEEL ONE,
OTHER TIMES YOU FEEL
24,900 AWAY
BUT NO MATTER HOW
MANY MILES THE
EARTH SEPARATES US,
I HOPE THAT YOU'RE
WILLING TO STAY

TO:

Love stabbed
Life's heart
And whispered
through her teeth,
"You don't get to
choose when you die
But when you do
you'll be thinking
of me."

TO:

TALKING TO YOU

IS A GAMBLE

BUT I'VE PUT

IN ALL MY TOKENS

BEAUSE YOU'VE

ALREADY SOLD ME

YOUR HEART SINCE

THE FIRST TIME

WE'VE SPOKEN

TO:

THE WEATHER

GOT WARMER

SO DID YOU TO ME

AND NOW YOU'VE

MADE MY HEART

SWELL TWICE THE SIZE

IT USED TO BE

TO:

SMILE ECSTATIC
AS ELECTRICITY,
EYES DARKER
THAN THE NIGHT,
I'VE GOT FIREWORK
DREAMS OF YOU
THAT WILL NEVER
LEAVE MY SIGHT

TO:

HEARING YOUR VOICE

MAKES ME FEEL LIKE

IT'D BE OKAY IF I WERE

TO GO BLIND

BECAUSE WHEN YOU

SAY MY NAME

THE THOUGHT OF HOME

NEVER LEAVES MY MIND

TO:

*IF I WERE TO BE
THE RICHEST MAN
IN THE WORLD,
I WOULD STILL
FEEL HOMELESS
BECAUSE I AM
WITHOUT YOU*

TO:

YOUR THOUGHTS

ARE IN MY HEART

YOUR LOVE IS

IN MY VEINS

YOU MAKE ME

FEEL NORMAL

WHILE GOING

INSANE

TO:

THE SADDEST THING

ABOUT HIM WAS

THAT HE THOUGHT

SHE WAS BEAUTIFUL

WITHOUT LETTING HER

KNOW

JUST LIKE PLANTING

SEEDS IN THE WINTER

AND EXPECTING THEM

TO GROW

TO:

(THE RAIN NEVER CAME)

> *MY HEART BEATS*
>
> *AT A THOUSAND TAPS*
>
> *PER MINUTE, AN EMOTION*
>
> *THAT CANNOT BE CONTAINED*
>
> *AND ONCE YOU NOTICE*
>
> *MY SOUL WILL BE QUENCHED*
>
> *LIKE AFTER A DROUGHT'S*
>
> *FIRST RAIN*

TO:

> *MY PARENTS*
> *FOUND LOVE*
> *MY FRIENDS*
> *DID TOO*
> *SO WHY DO I FEEL*
> *SO LONELY*
> *WHEN I AM*
> *THINKING OF YOU?*

177

TO:

LOVING YOU

WAS SHORT AND SWEET

JUST LIKE THE POEMS

THAT I WRITE

THE FIRST DAY

I SAW YOU I THOUGHT

YOU WERE BEAUTIFUL

AND THEN YOU NEVER

LEFT MY SIGHT

TO:

I KNOW WHAT

THEY MEAN

WHEN THEY SAY THAT

IGNORANCE IS BLISS

BECAUSE YOU SMILE

TO ME IN THE HALLS

WITHOUT KNOWING

THAT MY HEART'S

DISSOLVED INTO

YOUR ABYSS

TO:

NOWADAYS YOU ACT

LIKE EVERYTHING

I'VE EVER SAID

IS A LIE

BUT BABY THE DAY

I'LL STOP

LOVING YOU

IS THE DAY I DIE

TO:

I'LL GET OLDER,
I'LL GET WISER,
BUT IN A WAY
I'LL STAY THE SAME
BECAUSE NO MATTER
HOW MANY BIRTHDAYS
WILL PASS, I'LL STILL
THINK OF YOU
WHENEVER I HEAR
YOUR NAME

TO:

MY MIND IS EITHER

RACING OR I HAVE

NO THOUGHTS AT ALL

BECAUSE YOU

KISSED ME INTIMATELY

WHILE LETTING

ME FALL

TO:

A CITY FILLED

WITH STRANGERS

A SCHOOL COMPOSED

OF ACQUAINTANCES

A GROUP CONNECTED

BY FRIENDSHIP

A SINGLE SOUL

THAT I CAN CALL MINE

TO:

YOU LOOK AT ME

WITH EYES OF

CONVERSATION

BUT OUR HEARTS SPEAK

ANOTHER LANGUAGE

AND IT MIGHT TAKE

MONTHS OF TRANSLATING

GLANCES

BUT FOR YOU

I'M SURE I CAN MANAGE

TO:

I AM THE ONE THAT YOU MISS

ON THE WEEKEND WHEN

THERE IS NO ONE LEFT

ON YOUR MIND

AND YOU WONDER WHY

I NO LONGER SPEAK

AS I AM LEFT

IN THE BACK OF YOUR MIND

TO:

LIFE HAS MANY PROMISES. YOU'RE NOT ONE OF THEM.

TO:

YOU ALWAYS PLAY

ME A FOOL

EVERY TIME YOU

TELL ME MAYBE

BUT THE DAY I

MOVE ON IS THE

DAY YOU WANT

TO CALL ME BABY

TO:

$0 < X < 1$

*WE WERE PART
OF THE INFINITE
NUMBERS FROM
ZERO TO ONE
BUT WE WERE
ALREADY STUCK WITH
IRRATIONALITIES
BEFORE OUR
RELATIONSHIP HAD
EVEN BEGUN*

TO:

KISS ME LIKE YOU'VE
SEEN STARS ON A
CLOUDY NIGHT
AND SUNSHINE ON
A RAINY DAY
BECAUSE WE'RE A
THEORY NOBODY
BELIEVES IN YET
AND I JUST WANT TO
PROVE THE WORLD
THAT YOU'LL STAY

TO:

A THOUSAND PEOPLE

MAY LOOK AT US

AND SAY THEY

CAN UNDERSTAND

BUT KNOWING OUR

RELATIONSHIP

FROM THE BEGINNING

TO THE END IS LIKE

KEEPING A SINGLE

GRAIN OF SAND

TO:

I TRAVEL TO

ALL THESE BUSY CITIES

IN HOPES TO FIND

SOMEONE LIKE YOU
BUT ALL I SEE

ARE A MILLION

STRANGER FACES

WITH YOUR MEMORY

AS MY VIEW

TO:

EVERY OCEAN IS

PARADISE

NO MATTER HOW LOW

THE DEGREES

BECAUSE YOUR BODY

MAKES ME WARMER

THAN THE SUN

AND YOUR EYES MAKE ME

AS RELAXED AS THE SEAS

TO:

I KNOW WE'RE

BOTH YOUNG

BUT BABY WE'VE

GOT HISTORY

IF I NEVER MET YOU

THEN MY LIFE WOULD

BE A MYSTERY

TO:

I'M IN A CITY WHERE

THE ROSES DON'T TURN

RED AND THE VIOLETS

AREN'T BLUE

BUT EVEN

BUSY STREETS

AND HONKING CARS

SEEM ROMANTIC

WHEN I'M WITH YOU

TO:

YOU MADE ME AS

HIGH AS THESE

SKYSCRAPERS

AND WHEN YOU LEFT

I FELT AS LOW

AS THE CITY STREETS

BUT I GUESS THAT'S

THE GIFT AND THE CURSE

OF MEETING A SOUL

THAT MADE ME FEEL

SO COMPLETE

TO:

MY WORLD IS MADE

OF TRAGEDIES

AND WE HAPPENED

TO BE ONE

I NEVER FORGOT THE

LAST TIME I KISSED YOU

BEFORE MY EVERYTHING

TURNED TO NONE

TO:

WE ALL SEARCH

FOR THE FOUNTAIN

OF YOUTH

EVEN IF PERFECTION

DOESN'T EXIST

BUT IF I HAD TO FIND

THE WORLD'S MOST

BEAUTIFUL PEOPLE

YOU'D BE THE FIRST

ON MY LIST

TO:

I'M A WORK OF ART

THAT MOST PEOPLE

WOULDN'T
UNDERSTAND

BUT BABY YOU HAD

ME FIGURED OUT

WAY BEFORE

YOU STARTED

HOLDING MY HAND

TO:

*WITHIN A SECOND
YOU GRABBED MY
ATTENTION LIKE I'D
BEEN STUCK IN A LOCK
BUT WITHIN A MINUTE
I HAD TO LET YOU GO
BECAUSE STRANGERS
IN THE CITY DON'T TALK*

TO:

I BET IF I PUT
EVERY THOUGHT ABOUT
YOU AND PUT IT IN
THE COLORS OF THE SKY
IT STILL WOULDN'T
BE AS BEAUTIFUL
AS THE VIBRANCE
I SEE IN YOUR EYES

TO:

IT'S AMAZING HOW

OUR MINDS WORK

ASSOCIATING PEOPLE

WITH THE COLORS

OF THE SKY

BUT EVERY SHADE OF

BLUE TO ORANGE

REMINDS ME OF THE TIME

YOU SAID

YOUR FINAL GOODBYE

TO:

BABY I TRIED TO

SHINE FOR THE BOTH

OF US BUT THE

CLOUDS BEGAN TO

BLOCK MY VIEW

AND LIKE THE FLOWERS

I HOPE YOU'RE STILL

COLORFUL FOR ME

BECAUSE BABY I'M

STILL GLEAMING FOR YOU

TO:

WHEN I'M WITH YOU

I CAN FEEL YOUR EMOTIONS

FOR ME LIKE IT'S AS

SOLID AS GLASS

BECAUSE YOU'VE GOT EYES

THAT TELL ME I'M THE

ONLY ONE YOU'LL EVER LOVE

BUT YOU'VE GOT LIPS

THAT WHISPER THAT I WON'T

EVER BE YOUR LAST

TO:

PEOPLE TELL ME THAT

WE LOOK LIKE A WORSE

MATCH THAN WEARING

BLACK AND NAVY

BUT WHAT DOES FASHION

EVEN MEAN WHEN

I GET TO CALL YOU

MY BABY?

TO:

DID YOU COUNT THE SECONDS IN BETWEEN OUR KISSES?

IT WAS THE SAME DURATION BETWEEN THE INTERVALS OF MY TEARS

NOT VERY LONG AGO YOU TOLD ME THAT WE'D LAST FOREVER

BUT THEN ALL OF A SUDDEN TIME AND I HAD BECOME YOUR GREATEST FEARS

TO:

I INHALE THE
THOUGHT OF YOU
LIKE IT'S COVERED
IN OXYGEN
EVEN THOUGH YOUR
INTENTIONS WITH ME
ARE MORE LETHAL
THAN INTOXICANTS

TO:

**A LOVE STORY
ISN'T COMPLICATED
IF YOU VIEW IT IN
THE BIGGER PICTURE
AS FOR ME,
I PUT MY HEART INTO
A GIRL I LOVED
BUT WHEN SHE LEFT
SHE TOOK IT WITH HER**

TO:

I'D LIKE TO THANK

ALL THE PEOPLE THAT

SHE USED TO LOVE

BEFORE SHE FELL INTO

THE ARMS OF ME

WHETHER OR NOT

YOU BROKE HER HEART

OR THE TIMING WAS WRONG

YOU FORMED HER INTO A

SOUL THAT I COULD LOVE

SO EASILY

TO:

THE REMAINING PAGES ARE A COMPILATION OF SHORT STORIES, NARRATIVES, AND RECOLLECTIONS OF DREAMS.

BY NASH CONSING

DO NOT FALL IN LOVE WITH A WRITER

Do not fall in love with a writer, unless you are prepared to live forever in the form of his ink.

Do not fall in love with a writer, without the consent that you will plague him with years of literature, from the depths of your body to the bleeding loneliness he feels long after you are gone.

Do not fall in love with a writer, for when your relationships starts to crumble, he will try to convince you to stay with his own words.

Do not fall in love with a writer, for he will always have a record of the times you have radiated heat from your body, to the times your words have stoned him cold.

Do not fall in love with a writer, for he will always be searching for you, no matter how far away he may choose to push himself away.

Do not fall in love with a writer, because a writer may break you and you may break a writer, but you will never break his words.

Do not fall in love with a writer.

Do not fall in love with me.

IF YOU EVER SEE THIS.

SERIES

If you ever see this.

I had a dream about you last night. It wasn't the same dream I had before, where we would watch the sun dive into the ocean's horizon, and we would finally kiss once the natural lights would turn off.

We were eating dinner at a family event, although it wasn't your family, and it wasn't mine. It's like we saw each other for the first time since we broke apart. Or since I broke us apart.

And we just stared at each other. You were no longer mad, like the last time I remembered you.

But your eyes, the same eyes that used to spell the words "I love you" now drove stakes through my heart that screamed blood and tears of disappointment.

Without any thought, I screamed,

"I WAS YOUR FIRST LOVE!" in a tone that was an attempt to rebut your visual accusations of how I had left you without ever loving you prior to this minute.

And at that moment, the light blue fire in your eyes shrank down to a midnight ocean shade, a shade that is only seen when people are on the verge of death in vain.

I don't know why I dreamed about you that night. You hadn't occupied my mind in weeks. But after I saw the fear in your eyes, I knew that my words had treated you like bullets. Not only in this dream, but also on the night that I had ended everything with you.

But what could I do now? You were already far off, living in the world you always preferred being happy in, instead of surviving through the living hell that I gave you.

If you ever see this.

I had a dream about her last night. We were sitting upstairs working on a project for school in the tiny hours of the morning. I could tell that it had been a couple hours since we started. The fatigue started to come out on her face.

When we finally finished, she took a deep sigh, a sigh that slurred stress and uncertainty. The project must have been a big part of our grade.

All of a sudden, she stands up, takes a blanket from my couch, and opens a door to the platform of my roof. I watched her as she observed the night sky. I wondered what she was concerned about as she strained her neck towards the galaxies.

I then walked to the door and sat down next to her, wondering what occupied her mind. I looked up. The stars looked closer than I had ever seen them before. They winkled in an unknown yet familiar fashion. I wondered where I had seen the stars twinkle like that in my observing history.

The next thing I know, she leans her head on my shoulder. And for the first time ever, my heart sparked without intentions to, because I knew where I had seen those stars before. I had seen them in her eyes.

I turned to my right, only to see the galaxies right next to me in a girl's eyes that I had never really noticed before.

And by then, a class project had turned into a ceremony where two unlikely strangers told each other secrets by which only the stars in the galaxies had ever known about prior to this very moment.

If you ever see this.

I had a dream about us.

Or about you. I just happened to be there.

We were at a school dance. It wasn't my school, though. All of our mutual friends were there too. They were with you. I was on the second level looking and the dance floor before I saw you. I wasn't expecting to see you in my dreams once more. It had been a month since we last sent each other letters, and 6 months since we last saw each other.

You looked older, more mature. Not in a physical way, but emotionally. You looked like you had higher confidence than the last time I remembered, which was beautiful, because you used to complain about your flaws like these. But you were always beautiful to me. And as history would play its course on us, you would always remain beautiful to me.

Right before I went down to talk to you, our eyes met. Your eyes were still the windows to the galaxies. Or to the ocean. Basically, your eyes could teleport my emotions anywhere they wanted to. In that moment, your eyes told me that you wanted to be mine again tonight.

By the time I got to the dance floor, you were nowhere to be found. I looked for you in every individual, like searching through a seemingly unending forest. Ten minutes ago you had recaptured my heart, and now you were gone.

It's a funny thing when you see someone who used to have an emotional bond with you.

You start to question the universe with the same unanswerable question.

Why does the universe pair two people together, just to watch them tear each other apart?

If you ever see this.

Yes, you.

I had a dream about you last night.

I was with my normal group of people, walking through a school. It wasn't my school though. It was yours. I didn't realize it until I saw you.

We were walking through a hallway that eventually joined into a library, and you were sitting at the corner of a row of computers. You must have seen me long before I saw you, because by the time I saw you, you were crying. Tears of pain, tears of joy, I don't know.

I remember walking up to you. You looked different, unknown almost. But there were parts of you on your appearance that never changed. Like those eyes. And those lips. By this point I didn't know how to feel. I felt a quenching to a drought, I felt deep regret, and I felt complete happiness, all at the same time.

I wanted to hug you. I didn't know if you wanted to hug me. "Hey," I said. You said hello back in a way only you and I could understand.

You stood up and walked me and my group to an unknown destination. We ended up sitting at a staircase. By this time, silences grasp my throat. Maybe it did for you as well. That left us with small talk.

"How's it going?"

"How have you been?"

"What's been happening lately?"

All with the same generic answers.

And then the dream ends. And it's 6 in the morning, and I sat in my bed in the most pain my heart could handle, because the dream ended before I could even explain my side of our history, the side that you refused to listen to, and I just wanted to be okay with you.

OBSOLETE

You say I never tried.
You say I never loved you.
You say that I'll move on quickly.
You say that you are the only one who knows me.
You say that all I am is a lie.
You say that I am ruthless to your heart.
You say that I have poisoned your mind.
You say that I have broken your heart.

Maybe I have broken your heart and confused your mind. But do not ever tell me that I never loved you, or that I never tried. Do not ever tell me that I am a lie, because for Christ's sake, I have been spilling my emotions in ink for you like I have been stabbed in the middle of the night. Don't you dare call me the villain. Because I tried to save us.

But fate, dressed in hopelessness and impatience, told me in the middle of the night, exactly 6 months since I last stared into your eyes, that I could not be your prince. And like any boy who loved, I did not listen. But what good is it to try and deflect the ocean waves?

I am sorry.

Because I am not the villain nor the hero.

To you, I have become what I have most feared since the day I met you.

To you, I have become obsolete.

We were in class one day. I still didn't know your name. I didn't have to. Because you told me something that would occupy my heart like my own blood. You had given me a message, a message with no words.

People shuffled around, and you glanced into my vision, just as I did with yours. The universe automatically slowed down time, almost intentionally, like it wanted us both to take a look into each other's souls for just a fraction of a second.

It's an interesting thing to study dark brown eyes. It's a mysterious abyss, filled with more secrets than eyes which are blue, green, or hazel. In those colors you see the ocean, the forest, the earth. In yours, I saw infinite space. Space that included galaxies which held worlds where you and I bonded together like the atoms we were compiled of. Your eyes were a puddle in the moonlight in which you could see your reflection, but in a darker, more beautiful tone.

My eyes were just as dark as yours. I wondered what you were thinking about while you were looking into mine.

In comparison to the night, it is easy to appreciate the day. In daytime there is sunshine, blue skies, turquoise seas, forest hills.

But looking into your eyes, the eyes of a stranger, gave a sense of comfort to the own darkness inside of me. Because on a dull day in a gray school, your dark brown eyes happened to be the most vibrant thing I had ever seen since the last time that I had ever loved.

62814 – 12202019

I found a video of her while visiting old memories.

She was singing a song in a coffee shop. Instantly, my nostalgic mind transported me there.

I was in the back of the crowd. I could see her parents across the room, which made me nervous. She began to strum her guitar, and then looked up at me with the same familiar gesture that I had fallen in love with so many years ago.

She began to sing.

Her voice,

Her voice,

Her voice.

It gave me countless memories, like the time she would hum the tunes of our favorite summertime songs, to the time she whispered "Be mine." in my ear on a Tuesday afternoon, to the final moment when we spoke to each other, her last words to travel through my ears as "I don't want to go. Please, just hold me a little longer."

Hearing her voice made me think of a million different things about her. All the good things about her.   The song was a familiar one. I had to stop singing after the first few lines. Her presence was taking my breath away. The sound waves from her vocal chords kept crashing into my soul, as if my heart were a fishing boat being swallowed in the depths of a hurricane.

She would occasionally look at her fingers as they transitions between chord progressions, and then she would look up at me.

She was singing for me. To me.

The song ended. My heart's tempo began to accelerate as I became increasingly more eager to talk to her. The crowed began to clap. Her family applauded joyously. I took a step towards her, but she didn't see it.

She stood up and took a bow. God, she was so beautiful. She leaned towards the microphone.

"Thank you so much," she said shyly.

"This next song I'm singing is for—"

The video ended.

And like how a bullet ignites out of the barrel of a revolver, my mind was shot back into reality. It was exactly 231 days since that moment actually happened in that video.

Today, we no longer speak. I often think about other people. New people that I've seen around, or people that I've met. Beautiful people, physically and psychologically.

Still, none come close to her.

I wonder if she still sings in coffee shops.

If she does,

I wonder if she still sings for me. To me.

CHOSEN

In anatomy, our eyes are connected towards our brains. But emotionally, our eyes string a direct path towards our hearts. That's why first love exists.

As we grow up, our eyes are trained to define our own interpretations of beauty. We often fall in love with the wrong people. People beautiful on the surface, but if we were to see the emotional insides of that individual, we would automatically turn away.

Eventually, we find the right person to love. And when we do, our hearts are filled with the warmest and most fulfilling feeling. A feeling so addicting that our minds become so attached to the vision of 'the one'. The vision of the one we love is everywhere, from the faces of random strangers to the moment we begin so sleep every night.

Unfortunately, sometimes the right person exits your life. Someone so physically, psychologically, and emotionally beautiful, even possibly the most beautiful person in your life exits, with no words or with many.

After they are gone, our eyes search for them. We search for them in every stranger we pass, in every song we hear, in every story we read. Because by the end of it, we are not searching for someone beautiful anymore. Sometimes we are not even searching for 'the one' anymore. We are just searching for the feeling in our hearts that made us complete.

Some of us end up smoking our hearts full, or filling our hearts up with alcohol, but even after then there will still be an endless void in our hearts, a void from which we think we'll never recover from.

Until we see a beautiful person for the first time since we had a vacant heart.

And that, is where our story begins.

IRIS SUNSETS

It was the first time I saw the sunset in warm weather. The first time since last year. It's different, you know? Seeing a sunset in warm weather versus the cold. Warm sunsets always seemed to be brighter to me. More vivid. More rich. Maybe I was more connected to the world. Maybe I was happier.

Which is why I was sitting in confusion this afternoon. Because tonight was the first night of many warm nights, the first of many beautiful dying skies. But I wasn't moved by emotions. I wasn't connected to the world. I wasn't happy.

Yet it was the brightest and richest sunset my eyes had ever gazed upon. I saw rare shades of orange, purple, and blue. The colors were beautiful.

However, I didn't accept that they were, unwillingly. Subconsciously. Unknowingly.

Why did the most emotional sunset I had ever seen seem so unfortunately lackluster?

I didn't understand until long after the sunset that afternoon. I didn't understand even after I saw the same shades of orange again.

And then I realized.

Because we used to watch those sunsets together. I used to give you these sunsets, and you used to give them back. Since you were gone, I had every color of the sunset to myself. And it felt empty. Because I had every rich color, but I had no one to present it to.

But really, I saw no sunset that afternoon. I just saw colors in the sky. Because you were my sunset. You were the emotion. You were the connection. You were my happiness. But as their names call for it, sunsets eventually have to set.

And on that afternoon,

I sat alone in the night.

THREE OBSERVATIONS

A lot of the time, I find myself sitting alone, observing. Observing love, like the way two people gaze into each other's souls as if they found a nebula in each other's irises. Or the comfortable distance between two lovers as they wait in line.

I've observed this all my life, and I've had three very contrasting emotions produced, based on the stage of romance I've lived through.

The first time I observed love was before I had ever truly loved another person romantically. In youth, most kids found it disgusting, but really, on the inside, love was something that intrigued us. At least it did to me. The first people I saw romantically were my parents, and it opened up a new area of the unknown, just like noticing the universe for the first time. And maybe it made me a romantic, but after that point I knew that there was some point to life other than "being happy."

The second time I observed love was when I was the one falling in love. There's a lot more to love when you're observing yourself. You notice different things, like pulsating heartbeats, trembling fingers, the radiance of body heat, the feel of a first kiss, the contempt feeling of gazing into someone who you know feels the same as you. And you're so in love, that you stop observing. Because you start living for the first time.

And then it all ends.

And this was the third time I observed love. And the emotions I held were indescribable, but close enough to jealousy, hatred, loneliness, toxic nostalgia, confusion, and sadness. Because after the first time I fell in love, and after the first time my heart was broken, I had put myself in a glass box blocked off from the rest of the world without any opportunity to interact, and I was forced to watch the rest of the world fall in love as if I were brainwashed into having nightmares every night for months on end. There was no escape.

And I sat there and watched as I saw the one who I fell in love with, fall in love with someone else. The only thing I could do was scream internally until my glass box fogged to a point where I forgot about the trials and tribulations of love, romance, and observation.

But today, I opened my eyes. And I was no longer in the box, and maybe it might've been fortunate, and maybe it might've not been, but I observed the romantic world again. And I saw beauty once more. Beauty that I hadn't seen in the longest time. And even as my heart was still mending, there were dry cracks in my heart that were re-filled since my whole life had flipped around the cycle of love.

LOST IN THE SUBWAY

Our eyes met in the subway. Two souls paired together within the commuter veins of the city. Of course I didn't know you. I didn't know anyone in the city. It wasn't mine.

However, the city was yours. That's why you kept your hands in your pockets, your eyes to the ground, and your facial expression stagnant.

But you looked up at me.

Maybe it happened unintentionally while you were checking which station was coming up, or maybe you wanted to get lost in the tiles from a seemingly useless window in the railcar.

But when you took a glance at me, I suddenly felt the world revolve around just you and me. Call me a romantic. I definitely called you a realist. Maybe it was the contrast of the places we were raised, as I grew up staring at clouds and mountains wondering if the world reserved me for someone as beautiful as a stranger like you.

You however, walked past 10,000 strangers on a daily basis without giving a glance, or even a miniscule smile nonetheless. But you glanced at me a second time, a third time, and by then I knew you weren't just checking your watch. You noticed me.

Our eyes met, and automatically a decade's worth of fingerprints on the holding poles, the trampled wads of gum on the street, the solidity in the air of the automobile-exhausted streets suddenly felt irrelevant. Your soul was beautiful, and you thought mine was too.

But like all things at rush hour in the metropolitan world, moments like these accelerated to a pace that left my heart unfulfilled.

Because before I could catch your name, or more or less a smile, you exited the transit without a single thought of going through a deeper means of acknowledgement.

I would have become heartbroken, and I would have become restless in my sleep, but I learned quickly that

the city does not wait for romance to develop into crystals, it is manufactured at a fixture rate. And today was not mine or yours' time.

This wasn't the first time this happened, but at the end of the day, I did lose you to the power of life in the city. How I had lost to fate of the commuter system's slave.

My eyes were the only thing to tell you that you were beautiful.

And that, I believe, is the saddest thing to happen in a city with twelve million voices.

SCRAPING SKIES

One time, a guy I used to love brought me to the top of a skyscraper.

If it wasn't for his passion to impress me and his manipulative eyes that convinced my heart, I wouldn't have ever given the thought about riding up a 100-story building.

By the time we reached the top, I was already holding his hand. Maybe as the air pressure rose with the elevation, it pushed our fingers to become intertwined. The bell dinged. The doors opened, and a gust of wind whispered down our necks as if the ghosts of a hundred lovers welcomed us to the top of the romantic world. We were 850 feet above the earth. I looked him, and his eyes showed something new. Fear.

"Are you okay?" I asked him. His fingers were trembling, and his naturally pale skin looked like it was about to turn transparent. He nodded towards the edge, even though his facial expression had a contrasting opinion about heading in that direction.

We went to a corner, where the gusts of wind felt more like the waves of the Pacific Ocean. His arms, now wrapped around my body held me tighter with every step closer to the edge.

"You know, we don't have to do this," I told him. At this point, I wasn't even afraid of the edge. I was more concerned with him.

"I brought you here because I wanted to show you something." His voice shook.

I was confused.

"Why'd you bring me up here? I'm afraid of heights too."

He smiled.

"I'm not afraid of heights. I'm in love with the view of the city. It makes me feel alive. But on the other hand, falling is my biggest fear. I'm afraid of the possibility of plummeting to my oblivion, falling until I've lost everything I've ever had. This skyscraper reminds me of you. I'm in love with every view of being with you for the rest of my life. I'm in love with the way you pump energy into my veins and how you make my heart race to extremes, but I'm equally afraid of falling in love with you, because at the end of my life, I'll either be with you, or ill lose everything I've ever loved. You make me feel like I'm 800 feet closer to heaven, whether it's on top of the world, or if it's in the subways. I am in love with you. And I never want to fall over the edge."

AFTER HEARTBREAK

There's no formula in preventing heartbreak.

It's inevitable, no matter the magnitude.

You could be 13 when you walk into the school gym at the dance as you see that one girl who promised you she'd dance with you, dancing with that kid with the blue eyes. You could be 17 when your first true love says that maybe she is your first true love, but first loves never last anyway. You could be 49 when your loving wife switches adjectives and becomes your cheating wife. You could be 85, when your infinite soul mate tells you she loves you in her last three breaths. Heartbreak hurts.

Months later, you'll still think about her. You're just that type of person. You're passionate. You care too much. People tell you that you'll move on, that there are plenty of fish in the sea. But since the start you've known that you're a rare type of species. And when you find the right one, you'll swim away with her as fast as you can. Until she gets caught by the hook of a predetermined fate stopping a once believably infinite romance.

By then you get angry, and instead of going back to normalcy, you stay just as blinded as you were with love. But your vision shifts to hate. It's been too long since she's moved on from you, it's been longer since you lost your love for her. The only thing that remains between you and the thought of her is the feeling of hate. She calls you an asshole and you accept it, even though this isn't the real you.

You've got it all wrong.

You're too busy still trying to point the fingers. There are always parts of you that are always going to be complete assholish.

But if you're going to survive the disease of heartbreak, you have to remember yourself as the 13 year old boy who swore he was in love with the first girl he thought was beautiful. You have to remember yourself as the teenager at 17 doing anything for his high school sweetheart. You have to remember yourself as the loyal husband at 49 who spent 22 years of your life waking up to the most beautiful woman in the world. You have to remember yourself as the other half of a soul at 85 knowing that at any moment both of you will die, peacefully, yet in love.

Because we are defined about how we love, and not anything else.

THE PERFECT HEARTBREAKER

It was three weeks into our relationship when I knew I
wasn't the one.
It was the little things I saw in her.
Don't get me wrong, though. She was beautiful.
She had these eyes that were the color of over casted seas;
when she blinked I swore there was an aura of mist that
floated above her head.
She would hold my hand frequently, always unexpectedly,
which made walks with her through the hallway all the
better.
And when things came down to it, she always came to me
whenever she felt the need to clear things off her chest.
Sometimes she would burst into tears by the conclusion of
her venting sessions. I'd always brush her bangs out of her
face, pull her into my chest, and kiss her on the lips. That
always cured her stress, no matter what the problem was.
But had her imperfections too.
She was always self-conscious about how dull her gray eyes
appeared to the rest of the world. How they were the color
of a depressive state of mind.
She would let go of my hand too early, always after a certain
duration of time, because she thought that holding my hand
forever would make her seem clingy to me.
And when things a came down to it, she always seemed like
she'd only tell me half the story she experienced as she
poured her emotions onto my shirt.

She had the same number of flaws as the number of reasons
I thought she was beautiful. Because her imperfections were
the things that made her beautiful.

Theoretically, she was the perfect match for me.
But that was the reason I knew that I wasn't the one for her.

She was perfect for me,

But she wasn't my ultimate imperfection.

She wasn't you.

And all I ever looked for, was a piece of me that didn't fit.

All I ever looked for was you.

ADDICTED

When singers and poets write about their significant others and compare their love for them with paraphernalia, they usually go along the lines of "I am addicted to you like drugs!," they are usually referring to being so in love with their better half that they are in constant need of them in order to be happy, and without them they grow restless, like an addict who has supplied his bloodstreams in hopes that he will find his interpretation of "happiness."

I will admit that I was addicted to you like drugs, and your love did supply my heart with happiness, even if you did cause the destruction of my everyday tasks.

I depended on your love to find the colors of the world. Instead of picking the roses, all I did was kiss your incarnadine lips. Instead of listening to music, I just heard your whispers during our 2 A.M. phone calls. Instead of swimming in the ocean, I dove deep into the waves of your irises.

And after all that time, I knew we wouldn't be able to last. That I wasn't good for you, as you weren't for me.

And so like any motivated drug-addict, I made a New Year's resolution that I would take a path to curing my addiction. That I would move on from you, no matter how much it would dry my soul till my mind would be so brittle that it would crack and disintegrate for months.

In the first few days, I thought I could last a year being happy. Like any optimist on a recovery route, I thought I could be cured within the first couple of days. That a magical switch had been flipped so I could forget about every memory, every familiar touch, and every recognizable voice that had been embedded in my brain.

But here I am today, only one week since my recovery announcement. And I am experiencing a setback.

Because I am so in love with you.

God, I am so in love with you.

>And I cannot sleep or eat or move without thinking about you.

Because I am still addicted to calling you "baby," I am still addicted to dreaming about our future children, I am still addicted to being intoxicated from your released pheromones as I kiss the back of your neck.

I am addicted to you like drugs, even though the side effects include a hole in my heart and a disoriented mind.

Because without you, I do not know how to pick the roses. Without you, I do not know how to appreciate music. Without you, I will drown.

Without you, I do not know how to be happy.

KNOWING

How do you know when you're infatuated?

>When you see that girl for
>
>the first time in your life,
>
>on day one of University
>
>with eyes
>
>the same shade of brown
>
>as the coffee
>
>that gave you
>
>occasional heart palpitations
>
>because of all
>
>the life it gave
>
>to your nervous system?

How do you know when you're in love?

>When the girl you've been dating
>
>for two and a half months
>
>leans in slowly
>
>as she lays on top
>
>of your sauna of a vicinity
>
>and whispers in a voice
>
>that enters your ears
>
>but will never leave
>
>your heart,
>
>"I have a secret to tell you."

How do you know when your heart is broken?

> When your girlfriend
>
> for exactly a year and four days
>
> decided not to show
>
> at your anniversary dinner
>
> because she was preoccupied
>
> with distributing
>
> parts of her heart
>
> into the bodies of other men,
>
> sections
>
> that were supposed to be reserved
>
> for only you?

How do you know when you've moved on?

> When your ex love
>
> for somewhere around a year or two
>
> no longer shares
>
> the empire
>
> that infected your soul
>
> from the beginning
>
> to the end
>
> as a part of your life
>
> that lived from day one
>
> and died on day 369?

HEROES, HEART BREAKS, AND NOTHING IN BETWEEN

A COLLABORATION WITH

@queen.insignificant,

@uncoolpoet,

and @tricialwz

HEROES

by Nash Consing and Jess Heywood
Instagram username- @queen.insignificant

Love, is a beautiful thing to spread.

I swing back and forth along tightropes that connect lovers'

hearts together

and turn lost souls into found.

When people think of me,

they think of my arrows that pierce through their hearts,

and within an instant

they are shot into love.

However, my arrows come

as waves and dissipate through the heart,

slowly and wholeheartedly.

Sometimes, they come as slow as years,

Other times, they are faster than a bullet

fired from a pistol.

No matter the speed, they always reach the heart.

Except for some cases.

Sometimes, the ones I have paired

have already been injected of infatuation

with another person.

Sometimes, when I aim and shoot,

it passes through the head,

but not through the heart.

and sometimes,

my arrows only hit one person

as it misses the other.

The most painful part about accepting the responsibility

of having these flaws

is watching the ones in love

writing about what they thought was the idea of love

upon pages and pages

to only realize

that this was not the love that I had promised them.

And they look at me,

like I am the villain.

HEARTBREAKS

by Nash Consing and Alyssa Tirado
Instagram username- @uncoolpoet

It's not easy to have a profession as depressive as mine.

I watch over lovers and plant thorn-covered vines

that tear away the structures they have built

with each other in mind.

Sometimes, I perform a job in a matter of seconds

within two people meeting.

Other times, if they are lucky, I have to wait a whole lifetime

to slowly tear their hearts apart.

Flowers always die like days always end,

and my job is to remind them that love holds no difference.

The young have the most passion-

with intentions to last forever;

but I always find a way to make sure that they were never

meant to be.

The mature are the most complicated-

some linger on through years as they weave through my

attempts of separation

and usually I am successful.

The elders are the most difficult-

with bonds thicker than any negativity I can throw at them

because they have hearts built upon decade's worth of hurt

that has only made them stronger against my will.

Many go through me a hundred times before they die;

some only a few;

But the ones who laugh at me and feel unaffected

despite the fact that I have split their heart in two

are the ones that make me smile

for their courage,

for their strength

for their defiance,

against something

as terrible

as the Heartbreak

that I am.

NOTHING IN BETWEEN
by Nash Consing
drawn by Tricia Lee
Instagram Username- @tricialwz

I had ghosts. They were the thoughts and names of all souls that had left me, if they had the decision to or not.

Sometimes I would spend nights without sleep, because they'd be whispering too loud in the back of my mind. It's like they had conversations with each other. As if they were all friends. But they were all from different stages of my life, some from the very beginning, to ones that still lingered in and out of my romantic life whenever they pleased. The only thing the souls in the back of my mind had in common was that at one point, they loved me. And whether it was my fault, theirs, or none of ours, we were not together anymore.

However, on the night when you walked into my life, I was certain that every lingering thought that normally intruded my sleeping schedule had dissipated to a level of oblivion, a level so minute that even my brainwaves did not flow in their direction. Ever since we met, the thought of you had taken me away every night from 12 to 6 AM into a paradise that was higher than a dream, or a memory. It was halfway between the emotional layer of the atmosphere and heaven. The dreams I had about you, and the dreams lived with you were unlike anything I ever thought could have imagined to me. We were the "sweet dreams". We were "the dream away". We were everything.

But every good dream ends with a harsh reality.

And here I am, alone in my bed made for two, for the 43rd night in a row, with nothing occupying the insides of my eyelids except for the vision of you. Of what you used to be to me at least. It's strange, because I thought that as soon as we separated from each other's lives, you would just become another one of my whispering thoughts that you made me forget about. But those thoughts never came back. The only thing that lived in my dreams was you. Not as a ghost. Not as a memory. As you.

Because within a little over a month, I have become just one of your ghosts that you would soon forget about in the endless cycle of dreams and nightmares.

I have become nothing.

It's almost been a year since this book was published, and it's been quite a journey since then. The self-publishing experience of this book was mostly experimental, and I indeed learned many things from doing it. I learned that I am surprisingly terrible at spelling and at grammar, which are basically the essential characteristics of a writer. Realizing this fact, I decided to go back and make an updated edition of this book with all the typing errors fixed and all the awkward spacing at the paragraphs a little more regular looking. Also, I did forget to mention the fact that you *do* indeed have my permission to rip the pages out of this book and give it to whomever you desire to. But keep in mind that this book isn't perfect. It never was and I certainly don't intend that this updated version will be. These poems were all originally hand-written and raw, and so were the thoughts that came with them.

In regards to my Instagram account, I did realize that I changed it to the name that I've been called all my life, Nash Consing. The renaming happened at the end of the summer of 2015 after much thought and reflection that people wouldn't know who I was anymore. The reason I changed it was in fact because of the summer of 2015. I went to a camp called North Carolina Governor's School East, a five and a half week program for the core subjects as well as the arts, at a college campus with some of the most intellectual and talented people that I had ever met and probably will ever meet in one period of time. It changed me. The diversity of people, the mix of beliefs, and the different philosophies to learn about the whole world existed in a tiny area for a month and a half. By the end, I was a completely different person, but I was the same. I was Nash Consing. I wasn't just Nash in real life and @wyltbam_ on the internet. I had found myself. #GSE15

One more thing, Be sure to tag pages of this book on Instagram, Twitter, or any other hashtag using network with #TheMattressCatalog. Also be sure to follow my Instagram, the social network that made this all possible on @nashconsing. I always enjoy meeting new people.